SASQUATCH

INSIGHTS INTO THEIR LIVES AND ENCOUNTERS WITH HUMANS

KAREN E. MUELLER, DVM

Copyright © 2025 Karen E. Mueller, DVM

All rights reserved.

First edition.

Karen E. Mueller asserts the moral right to be identified as the author of this work.

Legal Notice:

This book is copyright-protected. This book is only for personal use. You cannot amend, distribute, sell, use, quote, or paraphrase any part of the content within this book without the consent of the author or publisher. No part of this book may be reproduced in any form or by any electronic or mechanical means, including information storage and retrieval systems, without written permission from the author, except for the use of brief quotations in a book review.

Disclaimer Notice:

Please note the information contained within this document is for educational and entertainment purposes only. All effort has been executed to present accurate, up-to-date, and reliable, complete information. No warranties of any kind are declared or implied. Readers acknowledge that the author is not engaging in rendering legal, financial, medical, or professional advice. The content within this book has been derived from various sources. Please consult a licensed professional before attempting any techniques outlined in this book.

Karen E. Mueller has no responsibility for the persistence or accuracy of the URLs for external or third-party Internet Websites referred to in this publication and does not guarantee that any content on such Websites is, or will remain, accurate or appropriate.

By reading this document, the reader agrees that under no circumstances is the author responsible for any direct or indirect losses incurred as a result of the use of the information contained within this document, including, but not limited to, errors, omissions, or inaccuracies.

Under no circumstances will any blame or legal responsibility be held against the publisher or author for any damages, reparation, or monetary loss due to the information contained within this book, either directly or indirectly. You are responsible for your own choices, actions, and results.

Cover Design: AI generated image of Sasquatch in the Pacific Northwest, by Karen E. Mueller, DVM.

CONTENTS

Acknowledgments	vii
Introduction	ix
1. WHAT ARE SASQUATCH?	1
Sasquatch's Physical Appearance	2
2. WHAT EVIDENCE IS THERE FOR SASQUATCH?	6
3. NATURAL SASQUATCH BEHAVIOR IN THE WILD	8
Sasquatch Sounds	9
How Sasquatch Hunt	12
How and What Sasquatch Eat	13
Sasquatch Living Areas	15
How Sasquatch Travel	16
How Sasquatch Mark Territory and Communicate	17
Sasquatch Family Life	18
Miscellaneous Sasquatch Behaviors	19
4. CAR SIGHTINGS AND ROADSIDE CROSSINGS	21
5. REPORTS FROM HIKERS	23
6. REPORTS FROM CAMPERS	29
7. REPORTS FROM HUNTERS	33
8. REPORTS FROM FISHERMEN AND FISHERWOMEN	39
9. REPORTS FROM HOMESTEADERS	41
10. THE FOUR MAIN TYPES OF INTERACTIONS WITH PEOPLE	46
11. DO'S AND DON'TS WHEN ENCOUNTERING SASQUATCH	49

Conclusion	55
References	57
Sasquatch Museums	59
About the Author	63
Notes	65

ACKNOWLEDGMENTS

I would like to acknowledge all those who have worked to document Sasquatch. From cave paintings to totem poles and other Native art, people all over the world affirm their existence.

Despite facing ridicule, many people have shared their encounter stories, for which I am grateful and from which this book was able to be written.

I hope that by writing this book, people who have had encounters will not feel so alone, people going into the woods might be a little safer, and people dealing with Sasquatch might find some ideas about coping.

INTRODUCTION

"Patty" from the 1967 Patterson-Gimlin film in Bluff Creek, CA.

Growing up in the Pacific Northwest, I was frequently exposed to the concept of Sasquatch, aka Bigfoot. As a child, I was fascinated with the subject, read everything I could find, and never doubted their existence.

At that time, there were only a few books on the topic and the internet didn't exist. The 1967 Patterson-Gimlin film of "Patty" striding along Bluff Creek, California, in broad daylight, had recently come out. It was so exciting to marvel at that footage, believe it was real, and imagine if there were more creatures like Patty anywhere else. Since then, I have maintained a lifelong interest in Sasquatch and continued exploring opportunities to learn more about this elusive creature. As a veterinarian and scientist, after a long and full career, I continue to believe in the existence of this remarkable being.

This book brings together information about Sasquatch from over 1,200 podcasts, books, magazines, YouTube videos, and conferences. Most of the information comes from listening to first-hand encounters with Sasquatch, told to moderators with personal experience. Because of the rich collection of first-hand encounters that have been gathered, we can now begin to describe, if not yet understand, many things about Sasquatch. I hope this book can be part of the beginning of documenting Sasquatch–not only in the wild but also regarding their interactions with humans.

The fact that you are reading this book means you are either curious about Sasquatch, cryptids in general, a Sasquatch researcher, or maybe just exploring new or different topics. In any case, I ask that you suspend disbelief for the remainder of the book. It will be much easier not to preface every description, statement, or story with "assuming Sasquatch is real" or "an eyewitness reported this, but it may not have occurred because Sasquatch may not exist." For the remainder of the book, please let us assume that over 1,200 eyewitnesses actually did see a large hairy bipedal hominid in the wild, something called Sasquatch, and reported things that I collated and am sharing with you in this book.

Please enjoy your journey to learning more about this mythical yet real creature. If you have personal experience with Sasquatch and want to share your story or need someone to talk to, contact a Sasquatch podcaster, a relevant Facebook group, or a YouTuber. There are many people who would like to talk to you and who will believe your story.

ONE
WHAT ARE SASQUATCH?

SASQUATCH ARE humanoid primate-like creatures existing in similar forms on every continent except Antarctica. They are called many names, including Sasquatch and Bigfoot, but also Hairy Man, Skunk Ape, Booger, Yowie, Wooly Man, and Big Bay-Ty, among many others. According to one paranormal communicator, their preferred name is Ayloyn. They are known in art and stories from almost every Native American tribe. Pictographs at least 1000 years old of large, hairy, wild families exist on the Tule River Reservation in California. Sasquatch are often included in tribal cautionary tales such as warning children to behave or the Dzoonakwa (First Nations name) will take them away to be eaten.

By all accounts, adult Sasquatch are enormous bipedal primates or primate-like creatures, typically 7-10 feet tall, and estimated to be 600-1,000 pounds in weight, based on the depth of their footprints and footprint casts made by experts in the field.

SASQUATCH'S PHYSICAL APPEARANCE

Sasquatch have been seen in many colors including black, various shades of brown from light to dark to reddish brown, and even white. White Sasquatch are sometimes described as "dirty white."

They are described by different witnesses as alternately well-groomed, looking like a well-brushed dog, to extremely matted and unkempt, with moss and twigs in their unruly and dirty hair. Their hair, not fur, is described as typically 4-6 inches long on their arms and shorter on their bodies. Their skin, which is often grey, is visible on their hands, feet, and face.

People have described their eyes as widely set apart and amber to yellow in color. They are almost entirely black with little or no white or sclera showing, mainly when they seem enraged or furious. When asked if they show expression with their eyes, some witnesses say that they have a blank stare with no expression, while others say they give a terrifying look that seems to convey, "I want to kill you."

Strangely, people often describe their eyes as "glowing" red at night. Witnesses insist the light from their eyes is not a reflection from flashlights, headlights, or any other kind of reflection but literally appears to be glowing. This phenomenon is often described by people familiar with the woods and wildlife, such as hunters. Podcasters frequently ponder this phenomenon and discuss it amongst themselves and with witnesses, yet it remains inexplicable.

Their mouths are enormous in size and extremely wide. People have described them as large enough to put an entire melon in their mouth at once. Witnesses have seen them eat whole oranges and apples in one bite and simply cannot believe how huge their mouths are.

Their teeth are often blockish, like "Chicklets" gum. They don't usually have prominent canines like dogs, but sometimes people say they have sharp teeth. Some witnesses report their teeth are white; others have seen yellowish and dirty teeth.

Their nose is most often described as flat, wide, and hooded. People usually say their nose looks like one that has been broken too many times, like a person who has done a lot of boxing. The insides of their nostrils are pink.

People describe Sasquatch's hands as enormous, almost unbelievably huge, described by some as like catcher's mitts. Their nails can be very long and dirty.

Their heads are often conical, but not always, with tiny ears that witnesses rarely notice or describe.

The classic Sasquatch shape continues to be reported as "no neck," which is one of their names. However, people think this is because of their tremendous trapezius and other back and neck muscles that give that appearance. This incredible musculature is probably also why when

Sasquatch turn their bodies, they turn from the waist up rather than turning their head and neck.

Witnesses sometimes identify the gender of a Sasquatch based on its mammary development. Like humans, they appear to be mammals that nurse their young, so they have similar mammary structures that are sometimes noticeable despite their body hair. Other witnesses have noticed Sasquatch with male genitalia during their sightings. Some people have seen family units clearly consisting of a male, female, and juvenile Sasquatch.

Their legs are gigantic, often described as the size of trees. Their upper legs appear to be longer in relation to their lower legs when compared to humans. This may be part of the reason for their exceptionally smooth gait. Sometimes, people report seeing a tree, which then moved, and they realize they were having a Sasquatch sighting. Their enormous legs have often been mistaken for trees in these instances.

Naturally, their feet are enormous. There have been Sasquatch tracks with three toes, some with six toes, and some with deformed feet. Many instances of baby and juvenile tracks have been seen accompanying adult tracks. Adult footprints are typically 16 inches long, but larger tracks have been found. Some of the biggest tracks ever found were 18 inches long and over 9 inches wide.

Their feet are also structured differently than ours. Much is made of the difference in structure called the "midtarsal break," in which the ankle bones are situated slightly differently, allowing flexion closer to the middle of the foot. This is thought to help give them the ability to push off the ground with much more force and leverage and might help explain some of the incredible accounts of their leaping great distances.

TWO
WHAT EVIDENCE IS THERE FOR SASQUATCH?

INVESTIGATORS HAVE BEEN TRYING for decades to collect hard evidence to prove the existence of Sasquatch, but until there is an actual specimen that scientists can examine and document, the mystery will remain.

That said, there are so many excellent examples of footprint and handprint casts that it is impossible to explain how they could all be from hoaxes. This doesn't begin to take into account the thousands of footprints, sometimes handprints, and rarely, even the print of a Sasquatch bottom, that people have seen and documented with photographs.

Of course, most people have seen the famous Patterson-Gimlin film from 1967 with "Patty" walking along Bluff Creek in California, which remains the most vivid and famous image of Sasquatch to this day.

Trail cameras are notoriously unsuccessful in capturing Sasquatch, but the Jacobs trail camera photos taken in 2007 show what appears to be a juvenile sasquatch walking on all four legs. There are some less striking photos and videos from regular and trail cameras in circulation, but it is still difficult to prove Sasquatch's existence with these in the absence of a physical specimen.

Recordings were made in the high Sierra wilderness in 1972 by Alan Berry and Ron Morehead, called the "Sierra sounds". Studied by the cryptolinguist (coded language expert) R. Scott Nelson, they were determined to be a real language.

Many other people have made recordings of what are suspected to be Sasquatch sounds, but it is practically impossible to confirm their origin.

Sasquatch investigators such as on the Colorado Bigfoot YouTube channel and many others, document what they believe to be signs of Sasquatch activity, such as tree structures and nests. These often take the form of enormous "X's" formed by crossed trees high in the air, or multiple large crossed tree trunks or branches mid-height or on the ground.

Lastly, in 2013 Dr. Melba Ketchum released a study attempting to prove through DNA testing that Sasquatch existed. However, the research did not hold up to the rigors of scientific scrutiny. Ultimately, more DNA testing must be done on exquisitely carefully collected and preserved specimens to accomplish scientific confirmation of the existence of Sasquatch.

THREE
NATURAL SASQUATCH BEHAVIOR IN THE WILD

A Sasquatch wood-knocking with a large stick.

SASQUATCH SOUNDS

THE MOST COMMONLY REPORTED NATURAL behaviors attributed to Sasquatch are their sounds. They make many different types of sounds--some more animalistic and some more humanistic. As mentioned, when studied by a cryptolinguist, Ron Morehead's Sasquatch audio recordings called the "Sierra Sounds" were determined to be an actual language. However, it is far more common for Sasquatch to make individual sounds or short streams of sounds than what sounds like a conversation.

Tree knocks and whoops are the most common Sasquatch sounds heard in the wild. Tree knocks are just that–knocks on trees. It is unknown if Sasquatch hit trees with their fists, knuckles, arms, or pieces of wood–probably all of the above. The sound carries quite far and can be extraordinarily loud. Tree knocks are thought to be a common form of communication among Sasquatch.

Whoops are sounds also frequently heard in the woods attributed to Sasquatch and thought to be a common form of communication. Whoops can be soft or loud and carry long distances in the woods.

Sasquatch are known to whistle, which has confused many a person in the woods. Whistling is not very commonly reported.

Occasionally, people report that Sasquatch mimic other animals, such as owls and coyotes. This would go unnoticed by most, but experienced people can tell the difference between actual animal calls and mimicry; the owl hoot might be a little too loud or have a lilt at the end, which gave it away. Many people report that they heard "owls" or "coyotes" growing up, but after they learned about Sasquatch as adults, they think they were actually hearing Sasquatch mimicry.

Sasquatch are known to scream, usually during an interaction with humans. Needless to say, it is terrifying to hear an enormous, loud humanoid scream. It is generally considered a severe warning for the person to stop what they are doing and leave.

Huffing is often heard during Sasquatch interactions. A huff is a short outward breath with or without some vocal sound. Sasquatch have incredible lung capacity, so their huffs can be large and loud.

Chatter is sometimes reported and described as sounding like hearing a conversation that can't quite be understood. Sasquatch sounds are also occasionally described as mumbling.

Sasquatch appear to use infrasound, which is used by several other animals, including elephants and tigers. Infrasound uses sound waves that are too low for humans to hear, below 20 Hz. Infrasound is often associated with making humans and animals fearful, anxious, sad, nauseous, or otherwise ill, sometimes for days at a time.

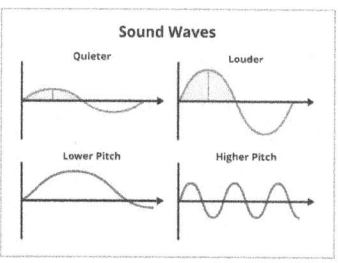

Infrasound consists of sound waves below 20 Hz in frequency, lower than humans can hear. Frequency is the number of waves in a cycle.

Sasquatch have been seen carrying deer on their shoulders.

HOW SASQUATCH HUNT

People commonly assume that Sasquatch are vegetarians and that they are found exclusively in the Pacific Northwest, mainly because "Patty," the creature from the Patterson-Gimlin film of 1967, was spotted there. These assumptions are flawed, as sightings of Sasquatch have been reported across the entire country for decades, and they do indeed eat meat.

Another common misconception, influenced by the 1987 film "Harry and the Hendersons," is that Sasquatch is a "friendly forest giant." However, thousands of first-hand reports of eyewitness encounters have shown Sasquatch to be aggressive and boldly seek food sources. Six-hundred to 1,000-pound creatures can't survive in the forest on berries alone; Sasquatch is a keen hunter and an apex predator.

Sasquatch often hunt deer. They are extremely fast runners and can chase down a deer. Many people have reported seeing deer run past them in a frantic and exhausted state, soon to be followed by a Sasquatch. It is thought that they hunt in numbers at least part of the time since numerous witnesses suspect they have interrupted their hunts.

Sasquatch are also strong and smart. People have found funnel-type logs or tree structures built in the woods to chase deer into for ambushes. Others have noted that Sasquatch breaks deer's necks and/or legs to disable and dispatch them quickly.

There have been many reports of Sasquatch carrying deer on their shoulders and reports of deer or deer parts lodged in trees. Deer are also found torn apart or gutted in association with Sasquatch, all of which require tremendous strength.

HOW AND WHAT SASQUATCH EAT

Native American Sasquatch investigator Thomas Sewid tells in his magazine *Sasquatch Island* of Sasquatch eating cockles, winter shellfish, clams, mussels, limpets, crabs, herring, rodents, corn, compost, poultry, livestock feed, and fruit.

There are many reports of Sasquatch eating from fruit orchards and gardens, and eating corn put out for deer.

Sasquatch seem to like sweet things. People who have established interactions with them found they love apples, oranges, and anything sweet, like candy bars. When they raid gardens, they usually choose sweet fruit like watermelons.

Sasquatch will rummage through food containers, backpacks, and coolers when entering camping areas. They will eat almost any food and drink nearly every beverage from any container, including alcohol.

Sasquatch have been seen crouched on their haunches, eating fish at the banks of rivers.

They have been seen eating raccoons. Skins have been found turned inside out as if "stripped" off of the body. One witness saw a Sasquatch eating insects with a stick during the same encounter as they witnessed it eating the raccoon.

They have been seen to eat the gut pile of deer and the entire deer itself.

Bone middens have been found on rare occasions outside of trailways or nests.

There was even a report of Sasquatch raiding a bootlegging camp and drinking large quantities of alcohol.

Sasquatch nests of branches and grasses have been found.

SASQUATCH LIVING AREAS

Sasquatch will live in caves when the opportunity is available. These caves are located along the sides of rivers or in mountainous areas. They have been reported in natural caves as well as abandoned mining caves. This is supported by the occasional presence of nests inside caves, a characteristic foul odor sometimes noted, and the presence of middens occasionally found outside of them. Numerous people have related terrifying encounters of hearing growls, screams, or huffs while exploring caves before making their hasty retreats.

Dedicated researchers who know what to look for have found nests many times. The nests that Kathy Moskowitz found in 2001 are well-described; one had three layers and a soft, spongy consistency. Many resting or nesting areas seem more like depressions in tall grass with or without boughs or other plants added.

There are many reports of Sasquatch taking refuge in old buildings like barns or sheds. Some farmers relate stories such as Sasquatch living in the shed at the back of the acreage for years.

Based on many reports, Sasquatch generally have migratory patterns, although some stay in one area year-round. Their home range can be extensive, covering many miles.

HOW SASQUATCH TRAVEL

Sasquatch witnesses have several unanimous things to say about their sightings: Sasquatch is incredibly huge, they are unbelievably fast, and they have an exceptionally smooth gait, almost like someone going down an escalator. For these reasons and many others, Sasquatch can travel incredible distances very quickly, faster than most eyewitnesses could believe possible.

Sasquatch are comfortable in the water and are strong swimmers. There are many reports of them being seen in rivers and lakes. They often travel along waterways, including into urban areas, as long as there is some cover to remain hidden. People who track Sasquatch sightings note that they are highly represented along waterways and that rivers and creeks link sightings from one geographical area to another.

Sasquatch usually walk bipedally but are occasionally seen on all four feet. It has been rarely reported that they exhibit a strange "spider crawl" gait, rapidly crawling on all fours and resembling a gigantic spider. People who witness this phenomenon say it is a terrifying sight.

Sasquatch have been spotted in trees and are rarely reported to travel routinely among them. Some reports indicate that certain Sasquatch are habitually found in trees in specific areas.

HOW SASQUATCH MARK TERRITORY AND COMMUNICATE

Sasquatch build structures with trees, and their structures are truly remarkable. Often, an entire tree is moved from where it was growing, carried or drug to another site, and crossed with another entire tree. Sometimes, other trees or large limbs are intertwined among them, forming a network. In some cases, "Xs" or patterns are added in surrounding areas to create networks of tree structures, sometimes with nests included or situated nearby. In others, entire trees are rammed into the earth upside down. Sometimes, the tree structures have more elaborate structures near them or extend onto the ground, often consisting of more "Xs." Nests are sometimes included in these elaborate ground structures.

Tree structures are visible for long distances depending on the shape, size, and time of year. It is unknown if they are territorial markers, but it is fair to assume they are meant to communicate.

Sasquatch investigators, such as on the Colorado Bigfoot YouTube channel and many others, are experts at finding tree structures and generously share their findings and interpretations on their channels. If you want to see what tree structures look like, there are many excellent photos and videos of tree structures available on YouTube. *

Sasquatch will often shake trees and break trees. This is most often reported in conjunction with human interactions. Tree breaks are frequently 6-8 feet from the ground, and the trees are often reported to be around 4 inches in diameter. It takes extraordinary strength to break a tree of this diameter.

Sasquatch have been known to build rock structures. These vary from small to very large rocks, too large for a person to lift. Their significance in the wild is not understood, but sometimes rock structures are left as a tribute for people.

*Start your search with the Colorado Bigfoot YouTube channel:

Colorado Bigfoot. (n.d.). *Colorado Bigfoot* [YouTube channel]. YouTube. https://www.youtube.com/@coloradobigfoot

SASQUATCH FAMILY LIFE

A good tenet is, "Where there is one, there are probably more." Although they don't appear to travel in large groups, there is usually more than one Sasquatch nearby.

During encounters, people often report hearing multiple Sasquatch in one area or coming from different directions.

People have sometimes seen mother Sasquatches with a juvenile or occasionally carrying a baby. Mothers have been seen to carry their babies on their backs and in their arms. Sometimes, witnesses will see a male and female Sasquatch together. Sightings of male, female, and juvenile Sasquatch family units have been reported in rare instances.

There are no eyewitness accounts of the birth of a Sasquatch. However, there is a compelling story in Autumn Williams' book <u>Enoch</u>, in which Mike tells of his observance of the burial of a young Sasquatch. It is a remarkable story that may explain much about their behavior and solve some mysteries moving forward. This book is highly recommended reading. *

*Williams, A. (2010). Enoch: A Bigfoot Story. CreateSpace.

MISCELLANEOUS SASQUATCH BEHAVIORS

Sasquatch are adept at braiding natural fibers. Tree limbs are sometimes braided into their tree structures. Small braided objects have been found in their nests. Occasionally, they leave these gifts for the people they interact with. They have even been known to braid the manes of horses.

Sasquatch are well known for stealing from homesteads. They will take anything edible, as mentioned in the section on what Sasquatch eat. They also steal nonedible items that interest them, like shiny things, marbles, and toys. Interestingly, sometimes these items will be returned.

Sasquatch have been known to steal clothing, and there are rare sightings, primarily historical, of Sasquatch wearing clothes.

Gifting by Sasquatch is a well-documented phenomenon. It will be covered later in the sections on interactions with people, but it is worth noting that gifting behavior is common. Whether or not Sasquatch consider gifts and tributes the same is unknown.

FOUR
CAR SIGHTINGS AND ROADSIDE CROSSINGS

Roadside crossings are a commonly reported encounter.

CAR SIGHTINGS and roadside crossings are by far the most common type of Sasquatch sightings. These encompass everything from seeing a barely visible entity out the car's side window to almost running into a Sasquatch in the road in front of the vehicle.

Sometimes, people have seen what appears to be a log or a stump, which suddenly gets up and starts walking or running. They will report that they could have looked at the "log" or "stump" forever and not have known it was a creature. Alternatively, the Sasquatch will be seen by a person, realize it has been seen, and go back to being perfectly still.

Strangely enough, Sasquatch play a dangerous game with cars. More often than not, with roadside crossings, the Sasquatch seems to time it so that it suddenly appears at the edge of the road, then steps, jumps or runs across the road in front of the car. People often report Sasquatch taking three enormous steps to cross the road and vanishing into the woods. Sometimes, they look at the driver of the car; sometimes, they don't.

It is exceedingly rare that people have reported actually hitting a Sasquatch with their vehicle.

FIVE
REPORTS FROM HIKERS

Hikers have often reported the feeling of being watched.

THE FOLLOWING ARE some common reports from

people who have encountered Sasquatch while hiking, usually in the woods:

Wood knocks and hoots: These sounds commonly indicate the presence of Sasquatch in the area. Hikers might hear these sounds while moving about on trails and in the woods. If you hear them, don't respond. Since the sound of wood knocks can travel great distances, it can be difficult to tell how close Sasquatch are. Assume they know of your presence and are reacting to you. It is advisable and safest not to engage with Sasquatch, especially if hiking alone, and to leave the woods if possible.

Foul smell: Although not everyone who comes near Sasquatch encounters their horrific smell, many or most do. It has been described in various ways, including a combination of skunk odor, feces, wet dogs, rotten eggs, and onions. The smell is so horrible it makes some people gag or throw up. The reek of Sasquatch has been described as peculiar in that it can seem like a wall of odor that people can literally walk into and out of rather than wafting like regular smells do.

In the book <u>Enoch</u> by Autumn Williams, the Sasquatch swam regularly and did not smell foul, except for one terrifying encounter with another Sasquatch. This suggests that regular bathing may prevent the foul odor. Another possibility is that being frightened may cause anal gland release with its characteristic pungent smell, as occurs with skunks, and to a much lesser extent, with dogs.

Unnervingly silent forest: Before an encounter, people often describe the forest, meadows, or trails as suddenly going eerily silent. Even the insects stop making their noises.

A feeling of being watched: This creepy feeling often accompanies having the hairs on the back of a person's neck stand up. Strangely, people who have had multiple encounters sometimes have this feeling before any other indication of Sasquatch, as if they have become more sensitive to their presence.

Throwing rocks: Hikers often report having pebbles, rocks, sticks, or pinecones thrown at them. They are tossed with remarkable accuracy, frequently landing at the feet of the intended person. Sometimes, these rocks are quite large and occasionally hit the person. Most of the time in these reports, the Sasquatch is not seen.

Terrifying scream: Oftentimes, the first thing that hikers relate in an encounter is a terrifying scream emanating from the woods. Needless to say, this can be the beginning of a nightmare. Assumably, Sasquatch is communicating their desire to have the hikers leave the woods immediately. Many people report that the sound of a Sasquatch screaming is likened to the sound of "a woman being killed."

Screams and roars that make your chest reverberate: Sasquatch screams and roars are often reported to make a person's entire chest and insides reverberate, and the screams last for an unbelievable amount of time. As mentioned previously, under Sasquatch sounds, people who experience their roars and screams at close proximity will sometimes report feeling nauseous, having to throw up, or feeling sick for up to several days or weeks, likely due to the effects of infrasound.

Rocking back and forth: When people visualize Sasquatch, they often report seeing them rock back and forth. This may be from nervousness, indecisiveness, or possibly frustration.

Fist clenching and/or finger twitching: Witnesses have documented Sasquatch clenching their fists or twitching their fingers, possibly in anger, particularly when they were being stared at. Witnesses were terrified because Sasquatch seemed like they were going to kill the person based on their body language and expression.

Seeing trees shake: Sasquatch frequently shake trees when they are upset. This may come after other behaviors, such as rock throwing, and may be a sign of increasing frustration.

Hearing trees breaking: Similarly, this may be a sign of frustration, anger, or rage.

Sounds of crashing through the forest: Sasquatch can be completely silent, yet they sometimes come crashing through the forest and brush like elephants. They may be showing their rage to intimidate people deliberately, or it could signify a temper tantrum.

Being "paced" out of the woods: Many people reported the terrifying experience of being followed by, walked next to, or surrounded by Sasquatch in the woods. As they tried to exit from the woods to their vehicle or home, they sensed something, or someone was walking next to or near them.

Some people described thinking they might be hearing a bipedal animal or person. They would try to listen to it walking–they would take a few steps and stop, then repeat, listening to hear it take an extra step after stopping, but it wouldn't be fooled; it would stop walking as soon as they stopped. This was terrifying, and they stopped and started repeatedly, trying to confirm whether or not they were imagining it. Some people reported catching it taking an extra step, and then knew they were being followed alongside the trail

Meanwhile, they had the creepy feeling of being watched the whole time. The "pacing" episode would often come after some screams or the unnerving silence of the forest.

Some reports detailed the last person in the group disappearing or being intentionally separated, targeted, chased, and paced out by Sasquatch.

Often, people would walk faster and faster or start running, and the Sasquatch "pacing them out" would keep pace with them, which was even more terrifying. Reports like these typically ended with the Sasquatch accompanying them in a frightening chase to the very edge of cover, then retreating back into the forest.

Many people who experienced this type of "pacing out of the woods" encounter were so terrified that they were convinced they were going to die. They were sure they would be caught and killed by the monster chasing them.

Occasionally, when people being paced out or flat-out chased by Sasquatches arrived at their vehicles, the Sasquatches actually grabbed onto or tried to climb onto their cars or trucks as they frantically drove off.

SIX
REPORTS FROM CAMPERS

Sasquatch will raid campgrounds, eat anything, and take things they find appealing.

THERE ARE similarities between reports from hikers, campers, hunters, and fishermen because anyone in the woods may experience Sasquatch's behaviors. But Sasquatch acts differently with different people, for reasons unknown.

Reports from campers include those from hikers, as well as:

Mimics of owls, coyotes, and other animals: Sasquatch are excellent mimics. Astute campers will recognize that these are not authentic animal sounds. Campers hear these sounds more often than hikers since they happen more at night. As mentioned, more people are starting to recognize Sasquatch mimicry, as they are listening for it now that it's becoming a known phenomenon.

Hearing bipedal walking: campers often report bipedal walking noises in the woods surrounding the campground. Unless humans are wandering around the campground or in the woods, this is Sasquatch.

Hearing rustling sounds at night: Sasquatch often enter campgrounds and walk around investigating. Many campers report withdrawing into their sleeping bags in abject terror until the sounds die down, falling asleep, and then emerging to a campground in complete chaos the following morning.

Seeing Sasquatch during nighttime bathroom breaks: There are many reports of campers seeing Sasquatch when leaving their tents to take a nighttime bathroom break. Sometimes, campers have seen great hulking figures rummaging through coolers; sometimes, they have seen them just outside the campfire's light, and one camper reported literally running into a Sasquatch.

Raiding the campground and stealing things: As previously mentioned, Sasquatch will take and eat all kinds of food and beverages. They will also steal many other things that interest them. One witness said that his full pot of beans was stolen--both the pot and the beans. People have had their equipment taken and batteries taken out of flashlights.

Hitting tents: People have reported many versions of Sasquatch having hit or slapped their tents. People have watched from inside the tent as gigantic Sasquatch hands have landed on the outside of their tents or arms have reached into their tents. Sasquatch have even been reported to urinate on tents.

Throwing rocks: Throwing rocks at campers is a common occurrence. This often happens to people sitting around a campfire when they cannot see well into the dark beyond its light. Rocks will land at or near their feet but usually not hit them, at least to begin with. People often think that they are being pranked by their friends, only to find out that this is not the case.

Sasquatch aggression: Some abandoned camping sites have been discovered that were suspected to have been left suddenly due to Sasquatch aggression. Sometimes, new-looking gear, including tents, sleeping bags, and clothing, were left behind. People have waited to see if the campers would return in a day or two, but they have not. No further information is known about these situations.

SEVEN
REPORTS FROM HUNTERS

Hunters have reported terrifying encounters in treestands.

REPORTS FROM HUNTERS regarding Sasquatch encounters may include the same behaviors as hikers and campers have reported, such as wood knocks, hoots, mimicry, or whistling. A hunter might also hear Sasquatch screams or bipedal walking.

Hunters might also experience the eerily silent forest, walk through a cloud of Sasquatch stench, or have rocks thrown at them. If so, hopefully, such a hunter would err on the safe side, pack it up, and go home.

Some of the details in reports that were more particular to hunters are as follows:

Sasquatch may change their expression and demeanor from calm to furious when they see a gun, especially if it's pointed at them. It appears that Sasquatches consistently react strongly not only to the presence of firearms but also know what guns are and become furious when guns are aimed at them.

Don't shoot a Sasquatch; they'll bring in their family and friends. There are usually more than one Sasquatch present, so if you shoot one, the other(s) will likely attack. Also, if you shoot at a Sasquatch, they may seek revenge. There are reports of Sasquatch returning in numbers and damaging people's homes and property, sometimes traveling long distances. One report tells of a Sasquatch traveling 50 miles to haze a person.

Shooting a gun may scare them away: Shooting into the ground to scare the creatures away has worked in some cases.

Stealing deer: Sasquatch have been known to steal a hunter's deer. There are numerous reports of hunters following the blood trail of their deer only to find it completely missing.

Stealing a gut pile: Similarly, when hunters have cleaned a deer and returned to clean up the gut pile, there have been cases when it has disappeared.

Deer were chased to the deer stand by Sasquatch: It has been reported that exhausted deer have run to the base of deer stands to rest, seeking safety from Sasquatch at the very feet of the hunter.

A Sasquatch reached up to a man's feet in a deer stand: There was a report of a Sasquatch reaching up to a hunter's feet in a deer stand, illustrated by the AI generated image at the beginning of this chapter. The Sasquatch eventually left, but it was horrifying for the hunter. He spent the whole day cornered in the deer stand, crouching in fear, waiting for a safe time to leave his stand and run out of the woods to safety.

A man watched Sasquatch eat a raccoon from the deer stand: This fascinating account described how a Sasquatch ate a raccoon while the hunter had a bird's eye view. This Sasquatch also used a stick to dig for grubs or insects to eat.

Hunters reported nausea and illness attributed to infrasound: Hunters have reported feeling sick after encounters, sometimes taking days to become normal. Symptoms included nausea, malaise, and depression, among others.

Trail cameras: Sasquatch seem to understand what cameras are. They can probably hear the sounds of trail cameras, even when people cannot. Trail cameras have almost never taken good, clear photos of them. Sasquatch have been known to remove trail cameras from their mountings, take out the batteries, break them, or otherwise disable them.

Hunting dogs were terrified: Some dogs wouldn't leave their owners to hunt once they smelled Sasquatch. Some got scared after starting to hunt, ran back to their truck, and wouldn't come out to return to the hunt. Others were so scared they ran away and found their way home much later, or were found after extensive searching. Some hunting dogs were injured and killed by Sasquatch.

Sasquatch destroyed the snowmobiles of men who were doing target practice. The men were shooting for a while, and then hazing by Sasquatch started. They decided to return to their snowmobiles, only to find them destroyed.

Sasquatch: Insights into Their Lives and Encounters with Humans

Make a Difference with Your Review

Unlock the Power of Sharing

"The greatness of a community is most accurately measured by the compassionate actions of its members." – Coretta Scott King

Curiosity and discovery bring people together. Those who share what they've learned help others find their way, just as one explorer's light illuminates the path for the next.

Would you help someone just like you—curious about Sasquatch but unsure where to start?

My goal in writing *Sasquatch: Insights into Their Lives and Encounters with Humans* is to present information about these elusive beings in a way that's both fascinating and accessible to all. But to reach more people, I need your help.

Most people choose books based on reviews. Your thoughts can guide other readers who are eager to learn more about Sasquatch.

Leaving a review costs nothing and takes just a couple of minutes, but it can make all the difference. Your review could help…

- One more person explore Sasquatch mysteries.
- One more skeptic question their doubts.
- One more adventurer prepare for discovery.
- One more nature lover appreciate the wild.
- One more storyteller keep legends alive.

If you love sharing knowledge and helping others, you're awesome. Thank you so much for leaving a review,

Karen E. Mueller, DVM

EIGHT
REPORTS FROM FISHERMEN AND FISHERWOMEN

Sasquatch have been known to throw rocks and sticks at fishermen and boats.

PEOPLE WHO ARE FISHING OFTEN ALSO GO

camping and hiking; thus, they may have experiences with Sasquatch that have already been previously described.

It has been noted that Sasquatch generally seem more aggressive with fishermen than with hunters, the assumption being that fishermen are less likely to have guns, and Sasquatch understand what firearms are.

In addition to the many other Sasquatch behaviors that have already been discussed, fishermen and women have reported the following:

Catch being stolen: One common report from fishermen and fisherwomen is that Sasquatch will steal their catch if it is left on the riverbank or shoreline.

Seeing Sasquatch upstream or downstream: It has been reported many times that Sasquatch have been seen up or downstream when someone has been fishing. Once they know they have been seen, they typically disappear into cover.

Throwing rocks: There have been reports of rocks and sticks being thrown at fishing boats. In one report, some very large sticks were thrown with great force that were potentially lethal and severely injured the person on the boat.

NINE
REPORTS FROM HOMESTEADERS

Sasquatch are known for raiding gardens and preferring sweet fruit.

THIS SECTION IS DESCRIBED as reports from homesteaders because usually if people are having interactions with Sasquatch at their homes, they are near wooded areas that provide significant cover, large fields planted to provide cover such as tall corn, or cultivated fields or gardens that provide food. Alternatively, they may live on farms near forested areas or other cover sources. People living in these situations will sometimes report:

Wood knocks and hoots: People who live near Sasquatch commonly hear these sounds.

Mimicry: People often get used to hearing Sasquatch mimicry of owls, coyotes, or other animals.

Sasquatch has even mimicked people's names. Creepily, one report described how a Sasquatch repeatedly called a woman's name, possibly trying to lure her out of the house. Interestingly, the Sasquatch always waited until her husband went to work before calling the woman's name. One can only wonder at its intentions.

Watching children play in the yard: Sasquatch seem to be fascinated with children. It is frequently reported that they watch children play, often hiding in cover and watching for long periods. Sometimes, they habitually watch children play, and the children are aware of their presence. Some children, now adults, report having told their parents about seeing Sasquatch watch them when they were children, and their parents did not always believe them. *

Attempting to lure children: On the other hand, sometimes there are reports of Sasquatch seeming to try to lure children into the woods around their property. They have been reported to make beckoning gestures.

Peeking in windows: It is not unusual for Sasquatch to be seen peeking into windows. Footprints are sometimes found in flowerbeds below the windows. Children may report a hairy man, monkey man, monster, or other entity looking in at them through their windows. When people go outside to measure how tall the creature must have been to see in, often they are at least 8-9 feet tall. This can be extremely frightening to children and manifest in them not wanting to sleep alone or in their rooms, by a particular wall or window, or in other behaviors.

Going on porches, trying to open doors: Occasionally, Sasquatch is bold enough to climb stairs onto porches and even try to open the door handle. Some people have reported having pies, fruit, clothes, or other items taken from porches.

Banging on trailer or house walls: This is a common Sasquatch behavior. They will often leave indentation marks on metal walls. The noises they make are deafening and can be terrifying to people inside. For some Sasquatch and homeowners, this behavior becomes routine. Some people report having their walls slapped hard enough to shake the whole house. Still others report having Sasquatch run up and down on their roof. This behavior is assumed to be a protest or angry statement. It can lead to more aggressive behaviors.

Throwing rocks at the house: This is another very common behavior. Some people report frequently having their homes pelted with rocks or pine cones, in some cases, nightly. Oddly, there are few reports of windows being broken.

Braiding the manes of horses: This is an odd pastime that is occasionally reported. Sasquatch that are near horses often steal the horse grain.

Eating animal feed, raiding the corn crib: Multiple reports have been made of Sasquatch raiding barns and outbuildings for animal feed. Sasquatch are quite capable of carrying fifty-pound bags of animal grain.

One farmer got around having his grain stolen by putting the bags into large barrels, which he thought were too large to carry. He soon found one of the barrels in the corral, about half-empty. Still, it was better than constantly losing his fifty-pound grain bags.

Sleeping in outbuildings: There are many reports of Sasquatch sleeping in outbuildings on farms. Occasionally, nests have been found in hay or straw.

Stealing livestock: There are countless reports of livestock going missing, with Sasquatch the alleged culprit.

Breaking the necks of horses and cows: Sometimes, there are reports of Sasquatch killing and breaking the necks of horses or cattle. Although this is shocking, it shows these creatures' incredible power.

Killing pet dogs: In general, dogs are scared of Sasquatch. If they sense their presence, they will hide, whimper, and not want to leave the house, for good reason. Pet dogs have been known to disappear when Sasquatch are bothering homesteaders.

Taking fruit from orchards: Sasquatch commonly raid fruit orchards. Many reports describe how farmers are baffled about where their fruit crops have gone. Since Sasquatch can eat tremendous amounts of food at once, it would eat almost the whole crop as soon as it has ripened.

Taking produce from gardens: They are also known to raid gardens, particularly for sweet produce such as watermelons.

Establishing a truce: Sometimes homesteaders and Sasquatch have established a truce, where they could get Sasquatch to stop killing their livestock or raiding their garden in exchange for part of the crop or being provided animal feed. One fascinating account describes how a woman provided a garden and horse grain for a family of Sasquatch in exchange for them moving her firewood.

*Always pay attention if your child tells you they have seen something like Sasquatch. They may be telling the truth. It is better to believe them and pursue it than to disregard their concerns. Children (and adults) who see frightening things can have PTSD that affects them for a long time.

TEN
THE FOUR MAIN TYPES OF INTERACTIONS WITH PEOPLE

Sasquatch will take food and gifts but it is not recommended, as they can be considered tribute.

OVERALL, Sasquatch seem to act in one of four ways with people, the fourth being the most terrifying:

1: Intimidating people and defending their territory: Sasquatch starts doing behaviors with the intention of intimidating people, probably to get them out of their territory. This might begin as communicating with each other, with whoops and tree knocks. It might then escalate to throwing rocks, sticks, or pine cones at people. They might also start hazing or pacing behavior. They might circle just out of sight of the campfire or slap the tents after campers go to bed. For people who live near their territory, they may bang on their walls, walk on their rooftops, raid their gardens or kill their livestock. All their roaring, screaming, chasing, and rock-throwing are likely based on protecting their territory and way of life. This is dangerous, unpredictable behavior from an enormous, wild creature, and it tends to escalate once it starts.

2: Gift giving and/or tribute expectation: Curious people try to lure Sasquatch by offering food such as apples or candy bars since they are known to like sweet food. The offering is gone the next day or at their next visit to the wooded location. This continues for a while. The problem with doing this is that while humans see this as gift-giving, some think Sasquatch see this as paying tribute. When one stops paying tribute to the apex predator, for whatever reason, things are going to go badly. There are numerous examples of this scenario ending in Sasquatch rampages of destroyed campgrounds, homesteads being invaded, livestock being massacred, and other chilling stories. Offering food to Sasquatch is strongly discouraged, as is all feeding of potentially dangerous wildlife.

3: Developing a genuine friendship with people: In this scenario, Sasquatch is curious, cautious, tentative, and non-threatening. They slowly develop a relationship of sorts, eventually a friendship, with a human or humans, involving gifts or tributes. This may go on for weeks, months, or years. It can include offerings of braided items, hunted animals, found manufactured objects, or returned stolen items. It can go so far as to involve the introduction of their mates or their young.

4: Wanting to kill and eat people: It must be acknowledged that in so many of the Sasquatch encounters, the survivors said they thought they were going to die and were sure that Sasquatch was going to kill them. The abject terror that people felt when they were chased, paced, tracked down, or attacked by Sasquatch is difficult to communicate in the written word. Many witnesses were veterans who had served, some were police officers, and none had ever experienced this kind of fear. Although these witnesses survived to tell their story, it is fair to say that some probably have not. It is not known if or how many missing people can be attributed to Sasquatch attacks.

ELEVEN
DO'S AND DON'TS WHEN ENCOUNTERING SASQUATCH

The forest is Sasquatch territory. If they give you a warning, for your safety, you should leave.

IF YOU HAVE an encounter with Sasquatch, DON'T do the following:

Engage. No tree knocks, no whoops.

Knocking and whooping in reply can be tempting and fun when you hear these sounds in the woods. Sasquatch might engage with you, and you can get a "conversation" started. However, what is the predicted outcome? They are apex predators who you are drawing closer, and you're in their territory. The situation may escalate, and you may become in extreme danger.

Meet their eyes; do look down.

Meeting the eyes of a primate can be interpreted as a challenge and is known to stimulate aggression. Since Sasquatch are more like primates than other species, err on the safe side and avoid direct eye contact. Highly social animals like dogs, wolves, and even humans interpret staring at each other as a dominance challenge.

Raise your gun at a Sasquatch.

Raising a gun near a Sasquatch may enrage them and worsen the situation.

Shoot them with a gun.

Where there is one Sasquatch, there are probably more. Your gun will probably not kill one, and their friends and family may come and attack you. Witnesses almost unanimously report that their firearms, no matter how powerful, seem unlikely to kill such a massive creature as a Sasquatch.

Antagonize them.

They may hold a grudge, and some have even followed people home to create havoc.

If you encounter Sasquatch in the wild or at your homestead, DO the following:

Leave the woods or vicinity as soon as possible.

Try to leave at the first sign of an encounter, such as rock throwing, noticing a foul smell, or hearing the woods go silent. Chances are good that things will not escalate if you leave at the first sign of the presence of Sasquatch. If you must leave your gear and return for it another day, do so. It's better to be safe.

Hike with others when possible.

Try to stay together and not let anyone lag behind when hiking. Sasquatch has been known to separate, chase, and pace out the person lagging behind.

Install outdoor lights everywhere that Sasquatch has been intruding.

Sasquatch will usually stay out of the range of lighted areas. They have been known to place markers such as sticks and rocks at the perimeters of lighted areas to remind themselves how far they can go so as not to be seen by people.

Install game cameras.

Game cameras may discourage Sasquatch from entering certain areas. However, they are known to disable, smash them, or remove their batteries. Purchase inexpensive ones- the cheaper, the better, as the noise from the less expensive cameras is considered part of the deterrent effect.

Share your story; you are not alone.

Contact Sasquatch podcasters, YouTubers, Facebook groups, or the BFRO (Bigfoot Field Researchers Organization). You will find an understanding and non-judgmental ear and that many people have shared something similar. Just telling your story, sometimes for the first time, can be very liberating and healing.

Read books about Sasquatch.

Read what researchers have found on the subject. It will reassure you that you didn't imagine your experience.

Talk to others who are interested in Sasquatch.

You may find other individuals through podcasts, on Facebook, or by writing or emailing authors that interest you.

Get help for PTSD.

People who have seen Sasquatch or have had encounters can be highly traumatized. Some people cannot return to their previous hobbies, such as hunting, fishing, hiking, or camping. Some people move away from their homes or never talk again to the friends who shared the encounter.

Please reach out for help if your encounter has negatively impacted your life.

**Please keep in mind that no one can be held responsible for the actions of wild animals. This advice is not a substitute for professional consultation; reliance on this information is solely at your own risk. **

CONCLUSION

Sasquatch are fascinating and mysterious creatures that inhabit varied environments almost everywhere on Earth. They are intelligent, powerful, resourceful, and cunning.

Through the firsthand accounts of witnesses, we are starting to get an idea of their behavior in the wild and as it pertains to people. This book is part of the beginning of documenting that behavior.

The fact is that Sasquatch are wild animals and apex predators. When you enter their territory, be wary, do not engage with them, and treat them respectfully. Hopefully, you can safely enjoy the wilderness without having an encounter.

The best Sasquatch sighting is one that is long distance, and from your car. That way, you can see them, but they won't interact with you.

If you enjoyed this book, I would appreciate it if you would give it a favorable review. Your feedback is invaluable, and every review helps!

Sasquatch: Insights into Their Lives and Encounters with Humans

Now that you've explored the fascinating world of Sasquatch, it's time to share your thoughts and help other curious minds discover this journey.

By leaving an honest review on Amazon, you'll guide fellow cryptid enthusiasts to the information they're searching for, and help others prepare for discovery in the woods.

The legends and stories of Sasquatch endure because people like you continue to share what they've learned. Thank you for being a part of this adventure.

Please log into your bookseller's website and leave your review.

I greatly appreciate your time.

Sincerely,

Karen E. Mueller, DVM

REFERENCES

Meldrum, J. (2007). *Sasquatch: Legend meets Science*. Forge Books.

Meldrum, J. (2014). *Sasquatch Field Guide: Identifying, Tracking and Sighting North America's Great Ape*.

Planet, A. (2014). *Finding Bigfoot: Everything You Need to Know*. Feiwel & Friends.

Williams, A. (2010). *Enoch: A Bigfoot Story*. CreateSpace.

Barackman, C. [Cliff], & Fay, J. [James Bobo Fay]. (n.d.). *Cliff Barackman*. Bigfoot and Beyond.

Colorado Bigfoot. (n.d.). *Colorado Bigfoot* [YouTube channel]. YouTube. https://www.youtube.com/@coloradobigfoot

BFRO Geographical Database of Bigfoot Sightings \u0026 Reports https://www.bfro.net/gdb/

Gerber, W. (n.d.). *Wes Gerber*. Sasquatch Chronicles.

Harry and the Hendersons. (1987, January 1).

International Bigfoot Conference and Film Festival, 2020, Yakima, WA

SASQUATCH MUSEUMS

To see Sasquatch footprint casts and other evidence, purchase gifts, memorabilia and chat with like-minded people, visit:

California:

Bigfoot Discovery Museum   831-335-4478

5497 Highway 9, Felton, CA 95018

Willow Creek China Flat Museum   530-629-2653

Highway 299, Willow Creek, CA 95573

Colorado:

Sasquatch Outpost and Podcast with Jim Meyers   303-816-9383

149 Main Street, Bailey, CO 80421

Georgia:

Expedition Bigfoot (The Sasquatch Museum in Cherry Log)

1934 Highway 515, Blue Ridge, GA 30513   706-946-2601

Idaho:

Idaho Museum of Natural History   208-282-3168

698 Dillion Street Bldg. 12, Pocatello ID 83201

Maine:

International Cryptozoology Museum

32 Resurgam Place, Portland, Maine 04102

Nebraska:

Bigfoot Crossroads of America Museum and Research Center

Harriett McFeeley 402-705-0000

1205 East 42nd Street, Hastings NE 68901

North Carolina:

Cryptozoology and Paranormal Museum   631-220-1231

328 Mosby Ave., Littleton, NC 27850

Oklahoma:

Chutay Ranch Bigfoot Museum   918-385-1148

202 Roberts Street, Talihina, OK 74571

Oregon:

North American Bigfoot Center   503-912-3054

31297 SE Highway 26, Boring, OR 97009

Texas:

Texas Bigfoot Museum 830-663-2532

North Polk Street, Jefferson, TX 75657

Washington:

The Sasquatch Store 360-327-3866

80 N. Forks Ave, Forks, WA 98331

Skagit Squatch Museum 360-755-0345

516 Avon Avenue, Burlington, WA 98233

West Virginia:

West Virginia Bigfoot Museum   304-644-0445

400 4th Street, Sutton, WV 26601

ABOUT THE AUTHOR

Dr. Karen Mueller was born and raised in the Pacific Northwest. Besides being a cryptid student and believer, Dr. Mueller has two primary passions in veterinary medicine: improving the lives of pets through reducing and preventing pain and preventing the single most common cause of death in companion animals: euthanasia due to over population. She has worked tirelessly in high-quality, high-volume, low-cost spay and neuter programs to address and prevent this problem. She continues to work in spay and neuter programs through the region, as well as practice at Mueller Animal Chiropractic. She hopes to help pet parents help their pets, through her new website PetHealthHarbour.com.

You can connect with her or see what's new at:

https://pethealthharbour.com

facebook.com/Pet%20Health%20Harbour
tiktok.com/@Karen%20E.%20Mueller,%20DVM

NOTES

www.ingramcontent.com/pod-product-compliance
Lightning Source LLC
Chambersburg PA
CBHW060533030426
42337CB00021B/4232